This book belongs to:

_____

Thank you to my husband Nesher,
and sons: Nathan, Owen, and Jacob, for still allowing me to ask
"So what do you think about this?"
Thank you Mary Ellen Fricke for her social media help.

Publisher's Cataloging-in-Publication data

Names: Asner, Carrie Sharkey, author. | Marzec, Monika, illustrator.
Title: Heart print : how not to foozle Mom's gift / by Carrie Sharkey Asner;
illustrated by Monika Marzec.
Description: Rockford, IL: Carrie Sharkey Asner, 2022. | Summary: Oh no! Every attempt at making Mom a
birthday present has foozled! How lucky that an accidental discovery leads to a simple, fun, and free way to
show love.
Identifiers: LCCN: 2022919256 | ISBN: 978-1-959175-04-9 (hardcover) | 978-1-959175-05-6 (paperback) |
978-1-959175-06-3 (Kindle) | 978-1-959175-07-0 (ePub)
Subjects: LCSH Birthdays--Juvenile fiction. | Mother and child--Juvenile fiction. | Family--Juvenile fiction. |
BISAC JUVENILE FICTION / Family / Parents | JUVENILE FICTION / Holidays & Celebrations / Birthdays
Classification: LCC PZ7.1.S48355 He 2022 | DDC [E]--dc23

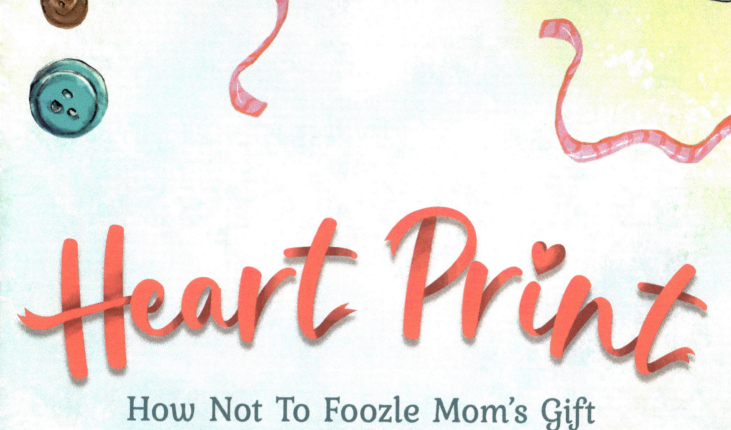

Heart Print

How Not To Foozle Mom's Gift

Written by
Carrie Sharkey Asner

Illustrated by
Monika Marzec

It's my mom's birthday and I'm going to
make her a present... all by myself!
But there's one big problem:
I seem to foozle everything!

I wrap bright pink yarn around a heart-shaped
piece of cardboard. I wrap and wrap and wrap.
Then I wrap some more. Only once does it tangle.
Mittens, just let it dangle!

Finally, I look down at...

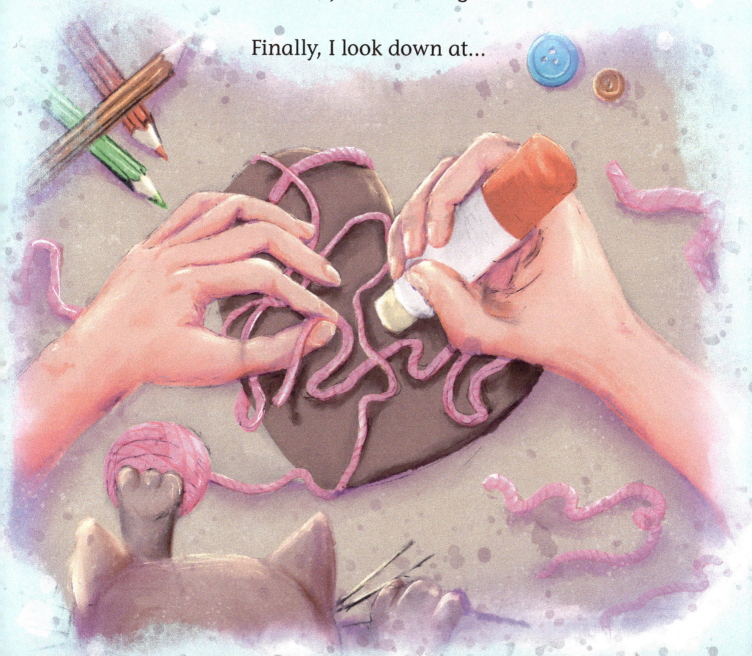

a bumpy, lumpy, dumpy mess! Oh, *Foozle!*
This doesn't look anything like a heart.

Sockeroo!
I know what to do!

I will dress up the heart with some pasta and leftover yarn.
I make a nice pasta pattern...macaroni, rigatoni, macaroni,
rigatoni... I string and string until all the yarn is covered.
Beautiful—a macaroni masterpiece!

I put it down for just a moment and—

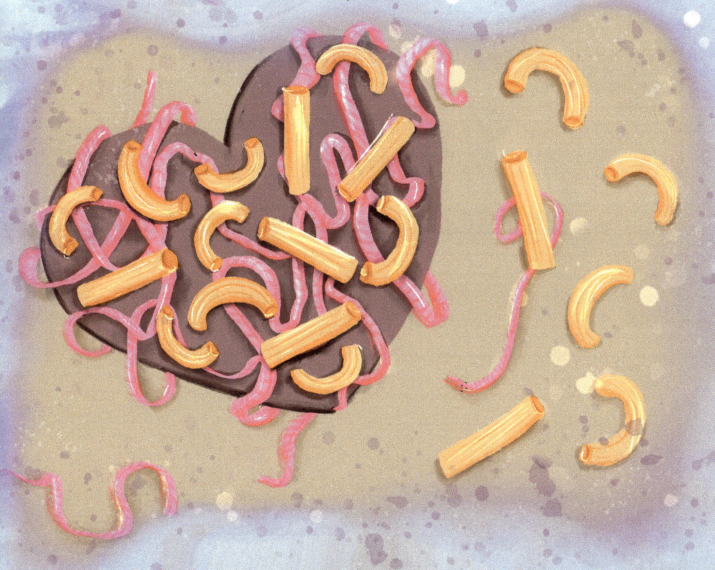

crunch, munch…
Freckles,
that's not your lunch!

Foozle!

What shall I do? I need to make
my mom a present.
I know!

I will glue these pieces of wood together and
cover the messed-up heart.
I glue and glue and glue.
I glue some more.

I try to lift carefully, but –

I get splattered with bloopy, gloopy glue
as the droopy pieces fall to the floor.

I am so mad
that I kick a piece
across the room.

Oh no!
It smashes right into my puzzle.

How will Mom know how much I love her?

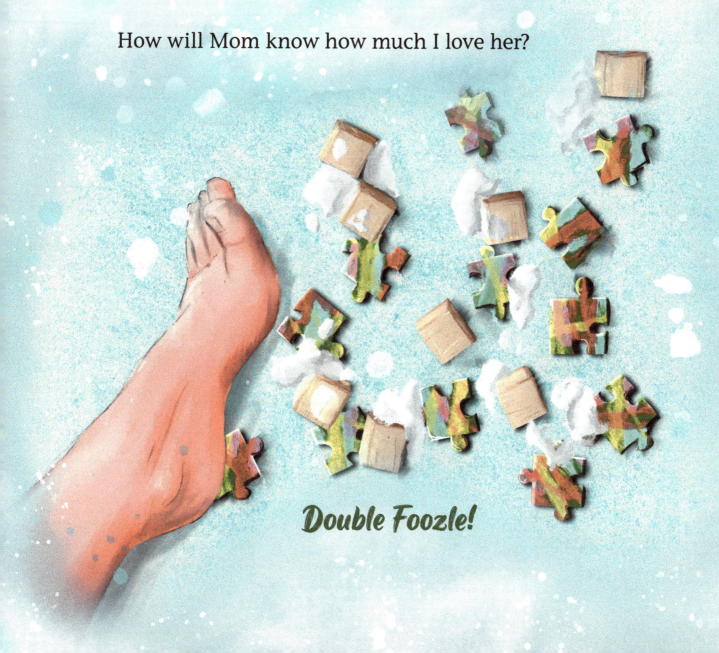

Double Foozle!

I jump when Mom's voice calls me to wash up
for grilled cheese lunch.
Grilled cheese is my favorite, but today,
I am so upset that I don't think anything
will taste good.
I bet it will taste like lumpy yarn,
dried macaroni, and glue!
Yuck!

I hurry before Mom sees the mess I've made.
I splash my hands under some water and
don't even bother to dry them.

I slump in my chair, put my napkin on my lap, and
wipe my hands dry.
Then...I see...a **perfect handprint!**

Sockeroo!

Now if I take my other hand,
and place it over the handprint...It makes a heart!

"Mom! I made you a present!"

Mom is beaming.
I can't stop smiling.

But as the water slowly dries, the heart disappears.
My smile disappears too.

Mom hugs me. "What's wrong?" she asks.
"Your present disappeared."
Mom smiles. "Your *heart print* was made with love.
It will always be there, even if you can't see it."

Sockeroo!

After lunch, we fill a bucket with water and
go on a heart print expedition.
I put one wet hand on the front door and
take mom's hand to make the other half of the heart.
Now OUR love will always be there.

We place our heart prints on my favorite things
—my plush pillow, my tattered teddy bear and...
my baby brother!

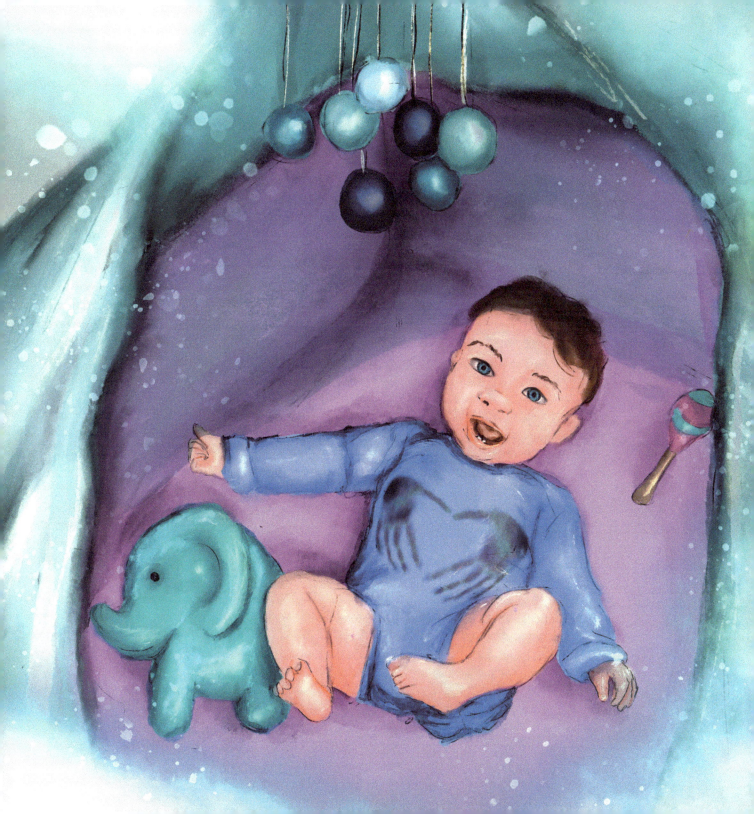

Outside, we mark my big kid bike,
the huge tree where I love to swing,
and even Freckles,
the macaroni-eating dog.

We make many heart prints.
On the sidewalk, we turn them in different directions
so they look like they are doing summersaults.
I do a summersault too.

Sockeroo!

We even make *heart prints* with our feet!

No matter if they are made with hands or feet,
our *love* is always there.

Mom says this is the best present ever!

Sockeroo!

Fun words that you will learn in this story:

Foozle

when everything seems to go wrong

Sockeroo

something amazing and successful

(These are real words. They are in the dictionary and everything!)

The Author

Carrie has more than her share of pictures of her 3 boys covered head-to-toe with paint, but she also appreciated the times when they painted with water instead. She hopes this book will show children that the best gifts between parents and children can be simple, fun—and free.

The Illustrator

Monika Marzec
www.facebook.com/mona.illustration/

Read Carrie's other book **Blueberry–Blue Bubble**. It is packed with humor, filled with lively alliterations, and is sure to have them begging to hear it again and again!

Visit www.CarrieSharkeyAsner.com for more information and book extras.

CPSIA information can be obtained
at www.ICGtesting.com
Printed in the USA
BVHW011223170223
658734BV00009B/806